Marty's Counting Adventure

A Hutterite Number Book

written by
Elma Maendel

illustrated by
Cynthia Stahl

Text © 2019 Elma Maendel
Illustrations © 2019 Cynthia Stahl
All rights reserved.

Reproduction without written permission of the publisher is prohibited.

Published in Canada by

Box 40 • MacGregor, MB • R0H 0R0 • Canada
P. 204-272-5132 • F. 204-252-2381

Cover design: Yvonne Parks

ISBN 978-1-927913-85-7

Library and Archives Canada Cataloguing in Publication

Title: Marty's counting adventure : a Hutterite counting book / written by Elma Maendel ;
   illustrated by Cynthia Stahl.
Names: Maendel, Elma, 1963- author. | Stahl, Cynthia, 1976- illustrator.
Description: Text in English with some Hutterisch dialect.
Identifiers: Canadiana 20190162007 | ISBN 9781927913857 (softcover)
Subjects: LCSH: Counting—Juvenile fiction. | LCSH: Hutterian Brethren—Canada—Juvenile fiction.
Classification: LCC PS8626.A364 M37 2019 | DDC C816/.6—dc23

Printed in Canada.

For my nieces, Abigail and Annette,
and my nephews, Terrance and Jakobi.
I'm counting on you for ideas and
inspiration for many more stories!

E.M.

For my Uncle David,
in whose classroom I illustrated
my first story.

C.S.

When everyone is busy
I amble through Lizzie's house
to look for crumbs and cookies
because I'm hungry Marty Mouse.

Delicious food is hard to find
to satisfy my hunger;
however, I discover something else:
the counting-world of numbers!

I race along the sidewalk
to Brennan School so big;
I join my good friend Lizzie
and we dance a jolly jig.

Together we make our merry way
across the road to the shop.
We hear **one** John Deere tractor
as it snorts to a startled stop.

Two of Lizzie's favourite people,
Olvetter and *Ankela*, dear and sweet,
invite us for a visit
and a tasty teatime treat.

Olvetter - grandfather
Ankela - grandmother

Out in the field where the wheat is ripe
three combines make their rounds.
We watch them gobble up the crop
as the grain in the hopper mounds.

Next, we walk behind the *Hennaheisl*
where soft mewing we can hear.
We find **four** fluffy kittens
that Lizzie thinks are really dear!

Hennaheisl - chicken coop or yard shed

As down the dusty road we dance,
we're startled when we hear a moo.
We clamber over the wooden fence
to pet **five** calves brand new.

Mike *Vetter* drives his Kubota past,
a cart is hitched to the back
where **six** *Klanaschuelkinder*
giggle and wave and snack.

Vetter - uncle
Klanaschuelkinder - Kindergarten children

The carpenter shop is just beyond,
nestled in the maple nook.
Seven newly-ordered kitchen cabinets
will surely please some busy cook.

On Fridays Lizzie's mother washes clothes;
eight full baskets—what a show!
We push the cart to the *Woschheisl*,
then on our way we go.

Woschheisl - laundry

Our noses sniff a yummy scent
as we pass the *Kuchl's* gable:
nine *Pfandlen Zwieboch* are set to cool
on the sturdy *Bochheisl* table.

Kuchl - kitchen
Pfandlen - pans
Zwieboch - buns
Bochheisl - bakery

Lizzie's dad manages the hogs, so down to the *Schweinstoll* we trot. We find a litter of **ten** pink piglets squirming for a juicy spot.

Schweinstoll - pig barn

Finally Lizzie makes a snack for us:
delicious strawberry jam
sparkling on a *Zwieboch*
underneath a slice of salty ham.

Zwieboch - buns

Yes, we counted our way around the *Huf* today,
numbering friends, machines, and more.
Now tell me what you can find to count
in your home, or school, or at the store!

Huf - community

About the Author
Elma Maendel teaches primary grades at Brennan School on Elm River Community, where she has lived all her life. Elma has been a teacher and principal at Brennan School since 1999. This is her third adventure with Marty Mouse.

About the Illustrator
Cynthia Kleinsasser Stahl has lived at Odanah Community since 2001. She and her husband, Herman, have six children, a daughter and five sons. Cynthia's work with children, both as a German teacher and *Essenschuel Mueter* (children's dining room supervisor), has provided ample inspiration for her artwork.

www.ingramcontent.com/pod-product-compliance
Lightning Source LLC
Chambersburg PA
CBHW080444090526
44586CB00047B/2474